QUIET TIMES FOR CHRISTIAN GROWTH

KELLY JAMES CLARK

InterVarsity Press
P.O. Box 1400, Downers Grove, IL 60515-1426
World Wide Web: www.ivpress.com
E-mail: email@ivpress.com

These studies were developed by the Thursday Night Bible Study, and the author would like to acknowledge the contribution of Mary Ann Avriett, Ken Ayoub, Gary Brinkman, Carole Geno, Kirk Kitchen, Jim Leibrandt, Nancy Mulbar and especially Betsy Wend.

©1979 by InterVarsity Christian Fellowship of the United States of America

All rights reserved. No part of this book may be reproduced in any form without written permission from InterVarsity Press.

InterVarsity Press® is the book-publishing division of InterVarsity Christian Fellowship/USA®, a student movement active on campus at hundreds of universities, colleges and schools of nursing in the United States of America, and a member movement of the International Fellowship of Evangelical Students. For information about local and regional activities, write Public Relations Dept., InterVarsity Christian Fellowship/USA, 6400 Schroeder Rd., P.O. Box 7895, Madison, WI 53707-7895, or visit the IVCF website at <www.intervarsity.org>.

ISBN 978-0-87784-176-0

Printed in the United States of America ∞

P	39	38	37	36	35	34	33	32	31	30	29
Y	18	17	16	15	14	13	12	11	10	09	08

PREFACE

Through the psalmist God has promised rich blessings for the person who meditates in his law day and night.

> But his delight is in the law of the LORD,
> and in his law he meditates day and night.
> He will be like a tree
> planted by streams of water,
> that yields its fruit in its season,
> and its leaf does not wither.

In all that he does, he prospers. (Ps. 1:2-3)
God's blessings are most fully realized in the person who works at delighting in God's law. His deepest blessings are not given to those wanting "instant" godliness but to those who are willing to discipline themselves to spend time with the Lord. Regular, daily, quality quiet times of Bible study, prayer and meditation take discipline. God then makes us fruitful disciples.

The quiet times in this booklet seek to challenge you to grow as a Christian in certain key areas. Each of the eight sections is designed to be done within a week. Since each section has only four to six studies, you are encouraged to explore the Bible on your own during the rest of the week to deal with any special needs you may have. Each study is designed to take about a half hour. Some may take longer. So don't be afraid to stop halfway through and finish the next day. You will want to keep a notebook of your findings each day. Writing out your responses to the questions will help you think more clearly, remember what you discover longer and so advance your growth in Christ further. Also try to use a good modern translation (such as the New International Version or the Revised Standard Version) rather than an archaic version that would be difficult to understand or a paraphrase that takes certain liberties with the text.

Your quiet times should also include a disciplined prayer life—a life of praise, thanksgiving, confession and the special privilege of bringing the requests for yourself and for others, and laying them at the feet of our sovereign God.

Delight in the law and meditate in it day and night. God promises that if we do, in whatever we do, we will prosper.

WEEK 1
THE CHARACTER OF GOD

QUIET TIME 1. KNOWING GOD

Pray to the God who can be known, who out of his love has revealed himself to you. Confess your sins to clear the air between you and God. Ask him to give you a quiet mind and to direct your thoughts to him.

Read Genesis 17:1-8. **1.** How is God described in verse 1? **2.** Who took the initiative in establishing the relationship between God and Abraham? What does that tell you about God? **3.** Look up *covenant* (see v. 2) in a dictionary. **4.** What conditions of the covenant between Abraham and God did Abraham have to satisfy? What does it mean to walk before God? **5.** What promises did God give Abraham? **6.** In verse 7 the emphasis switches from Abraham to his descendants. Although we aren't direct descendants of Abraham, we do take part in a covenant with God through Jesus Christ. What promise did God give to Abraham's descendants? How long will the covenant last? **7.** What does it mean to you that God is God to you? **8.** What implications does that have for your life (see v. 1)? **9.** We see that God has freely chosen to reveal himself to us. He is a God who can be known and who has established a relationship with his people. What's the difference between knowing someone and knowing *about* someone? between knowing God and knowing about God? **10.** What does a relationship with someone involve? **11.** How can you get to know God better and improve your relationship with him?

Pray to the God who is God to you that you might know him better.

QUIET TIME 2. THE FATHER

Pray: Ask God to give you a mind centered on him. Ask him to teach you who he is.

Read Hosea 11:1-9. **1.** What is the special relationship given to the nation of Israel as described in verses 1-7? **2.** What images here show God's fatherlike love? **3.** How should children react to such gentle care? **4.** How did God's chosen people react? **5.** Summarize the well-deserved punishment God describes in verses 5-7. **6.** In verses 8-9, Ephraim (one of the northern tribes of Israel) represents the whole nation. Admah and Zeboiim are associated with Sodom and Gomorrah. How does God describe himself here? **7.** What does *holy* mean? (Try a dictionary if you need to.) **8.** How should we, who have many attitudes similar to those of his chosen ones described here, feel when approaching a holy God? **9.** Why does God decide against the complete destruction of the rebellious people he had blessed so well? **10.** In what ways have you been "bent on turning away from" God (v. 7)? What do you need to do about that?

Pray: Praise God that he is such a Father to us and that he has chosen you. Thank him for his mercy to you and your need for his guidance and compassion.

QUIET TIME 3. JESUS CHRIST

Pray that you might know more fully the only true God and Jesus Christ whom he sent.

Read Colossians 1:15-22. **1.** This is one of the most important passages in the Bible revealing the character of Jesus Christ. In your notebook make two columns. In the first, list everything this passage teaches about who Jesus is. In the second column list what he has done. **2.** For each column, write a paragraph on what the phrases you listed mean. **3.** Can you trust the Jesus who is revealed in this passage? **4.** In which areas do you feel it is most difficult to trust him? Why? **5.** Think of who Jesus is and what he does. What do you find most encouraging and why? **6.** What do you need to start doing to allow this Jesus to work in your life?

Pray: Turn over to God the areas listed in question 4. Thank him for the encouragement that he has given you in Jesus Christ. Open up your life to Jesus to allow him to work in it.

QUIET TIME 4. THE HOLY SPIRIT

Pray: Clear the air with God and ask him to guide your thoughts to him.

Read Romans 8:1-17. **1.** The Holy Spirit makes the connection between us and Christ's work on the cross. What results from that connection according to verses 1-2? **2.** What does it mean to walk according to the Spirit (v. 4)? How does that differ from walking according to the flesh? **3.** According to verses 5-7 how has the Holy Spirit changed our relationship with God? What are some characteristics of this new relationship? **4.** What benefits do we receive through the Spirit according to verses 9-11? **5.** Jesus has called us to live a new life of obedience. Because we've been set free from the bondage of sin by the Holy Spirit we are free to be obedient by the Spirit's power. The New American Standard Bible translates verses 12-14 as, "We are under obligation, not . . . to live according to the flesh" but to be led by the Spirit of God. How important does this make our actions in the new life? **6.** How does the Holy Spirit assure us of our adoption into the family of God (vv. 14-16)? **7.** What does it mean to be an heir? (A dictionary could help.) What special benefits will we inherit by being heirs of God (v. 17)? **8.** God is working to make us more godly. When he finishes, we will be glorified, that is transformed into the perfect image of Jesus Christ. This process toward holiness is called sanctification. The Holy Spirit has begun and will complete that process. Where has God been changing your life?

Pray: Thank God for the surprising gift of his Holy Spirit. Thank him also for all the benefits that have been given to you through his Spirit. Pray that the Spirit will continue to change the areas of your life he has begun to transform.

QUIET TIME 5. LIFE IN CHRIST
Pray that God will show you the riches of your life in Christ.

Read Colossians 2:6-15. **1.** What are we commanded to do in verses 6-7? **2.** How is Christ described in verse 9? **3.** What do we have according to verse 10? What do you think that means?

4. Verses 11-12 say that we were circumcised, in the putting off of our sinful nature. This is a figurative expression describing the cutting off of our old sinful nature which the Bible calls the flesh. What do you think it means to be buried and raised with Christ (remembering that this paragraph is discussing our old, sinful nature)? **5.** Describe what God has done for us according to verse 13. **6.** Describe how God has done that for us (vv. 14-15). **7.** Look carefully over the passage you just studied. Now write a prayer to God describing your thankfulness for all that he has done for you in Jesus Christ. (Remember v. 7: we are to be "abounding in thanksgiving.")

QUIET TIME 6. SEPARATION FROM GOD

Pray that God will illumine to you who you are in relationship to him.

Read Romans 1:18-32. **1.** What does God reveal toward humanity? **2.** This passage teaches how people have provoked God's wrath. How has God revealed himself to everyone? What can we know of God through creation? **3.** What did people do with that knowledge (v. 21)? Why would not honoring God be such an extremely serious offense? **4.** When people give up the rightful worship of their Creator, whom do they begin to worship (v. 25)? **5.** The root of sin is failing to honor God. Some use the word *rebellion* to describe this state. Why would this be a good word to use? **6.** Sin, as rebellion against God's rightful authority over his creatures, can be evidenced in a variety of ways. List those mentioned in verses 26-32. If you don't know the meaning of some of the sins listed, write down their definitions from a dictionary. **7.** Which of the acts and attitudes listed in verses 26-31 are you most guilty of? Confess these now. **8.** Write a short paragraph summarizing why we have incurred God's wrath and how we got into that state. **9.** The Scripture teach that all have sinned (Rom. 6:23) and that the only way to establish a right relationship with God is through faith in Jesus Christ. If you are not sure that you have turned from your sins and begun trusting in Jesus Christ for forgiveness of your sins, talk to a Christian friend or read *Becoming a Christian* by John R. W. Stott (IVP).

Further study: Getting to Know God by Paul Steeves (IVP).

WEEK 2
PRAYER

QUIET TIME 1. COMMUNICATING WITH GOD

Pray: Ask for a clear, calm and open mind. Ask him to teach you today.

Jacob and Esau were twins. Although all the family property and the blessing of their father Issac belonged to Esau, the first-born, Jacob stole the birthright through trickery. He was then driven into a distant country by his furious brother. After many years in exile, Jacob was told by God that he should return and that he would be with him continually. Still frightened by the anger of his brother, Jacob returned with all the wealth he had acquired while away.

Read Genesis 32:3-12. **1.** Why does Jacob send messengers to Esau? **2.** How does Jacob feel about what the messengers tell him (vv. 6-7)? Why? **3.** Whom does Jacob call on in his time of need? We often pray when we're in trouble. What are some other reasons for prayer? **4.** What are some differences between Jacob's conversation with God (vv. 9-12) and one with any other person? What are the similarities? **5.** How could your prayers be more natural and conversational? **6.** Not only do people desire to talk to God, but God has made an effort to establish relationships with us. What relationships does Jacob remember in verse 9? **7.** What has God done for Jacob (v. 10)? **8.** What does Jacob know about his worthiness to receive gifts or ask for help? **9.** Though he knows that God isn't obligated to answer, what does Jacob ask for in verse 11? **10.** Why is it important to approach God in a humble, open manner? **11.** What promise supports Jacob's hope that he will be rescued? Read two promises found in 1 Peter 5:6-7.

Pray: Talk with the personal God who has given you these promises.

QUIET TIME 2. ELEMENTS OF PRAYER

Pray: Ask God to guide your thoughts to him.

1. From the following verses, list four different elements which should be a part of our prayer life: Psalm 22:23; 1 Thessalonians 5:18; 1 John 1:9; Ephesians 6:18. **2.** Describe briefly each of these kinds of prayer. **3.** Why are each of these elements important to God and to you? **4.** List these four elements of prayer once more. Write down specific prayers under each category which are important to you. Think: What can I praise God for, thank him for, confess to him and ask for help? Keep this prayer list and add to it regularly. It will help you persevere in prayer, be organized, remember to thank God for answers, and show you that he does hear us and respond.

Pray: Take some extra time to pray using your list.

QUIET TIME 3. FAITH IN PRAYER

Pray: Ask God to teach you more about his faithfulness and generosity.

Read James 1:5-8. **1.** What does James tell us about God's character in these verses? **2.** What words and images does he use to describe those who pray without faith? **3.** How effective are faithless prayers? **4.** Keeping verse 6 in mind, write a short definition of faith. **5.** Faith without doubt is not unusual. Christians base their faith on the historical evidence for the resurrection of Christ which substantiates his claims to be God's Son. Because Christ rose, we can trust that he will answer our prayers as he promised. How does a knowledge of God's character (such as what is mentioned in v. 5) help you to know that God will answer your prayers? **6.** How effective are prayers with faith (v. 5)? **7.** What prayers have you prayed recently without believing completely that results are possible? **8.** How can you change your prayers so that you believe they will be answered?

Pray: Specific, bite-sized requests can be better to start with than huge, general requests if your faith can only chew small pieces. Look at your list of requests from yesterday's quiet time and revise them, if you need to, to make them more specific and believable. Now pray about these knowing that if you ask in faith, without doubting, that God will answer you.

QUIET TIME 4. GOD'S WILL IN PRAYER

Pray that God will make you willing to obey him.

Read 1 John 5:14-15. **1.** What confidence before God does John say we have when we pray according to his will? **2.** Why is it important to pray according to his will? **3.** We know that God is all-knowing and that he loves us. How should this affect our attitude toward his will? **4.** What might cause us to resist his will? **5.** Look over your revised prayer list. Does each prayer conform to the knowledge you have of God's will? **6.** How might you check to see if your requests conform to God's will?

Pray: Ask God to make his will clear to you as you examine your prayer list.

QUIET TIME 5. UNANSWERED PRAYER

Pray: Ask God to fill you with his Holy Spirit and guide you into his truth.

1. There are several reasons for unanswered prayer: What does James 4:3 say about wrong motives in asking? **2.** Read 1 John 3:21-23. What is meant by the reference in verse 21 to our hearts condemning us? How does a condemning heart affect our relationship with God? **3.** If our hearts don't condemn us, what assurance do we have in prayer? **4.** What is required of us? What two commandments are mentioned here? **5.** Look over your prayer list. Which seem unanswered? Check your motives in praying. Check for sin in your life that God may desire to bring to your attention. If your heart is clear, perhaps the answer to your prayer is being kept for the best time and you must patiently continue to pray to God with confidence.

Pray: Ask God to help you understand some of the reasons that he is withholding answers. Ask him for confidence as you pray. Thank him for the answers he has already given.

Further reading: Prayer by O. Hallesby (Augsburg); *If You Haven't Got a Prayer* by Crotts (IVP).

WEEK 3
FELLOWSHIP

QUIET TIME 1. MEETING TOGETHER

Pray: Ask God to teach you the importance of fellowship with other Christians.

Read Hebrews 10:23-25. **1.** What are we to hold fast to? **2.** In what is our hope? **3.** What enables us to "hold fast . . . without wavering" to the object of our hope? **4.** What we learn in verse 23 provides the basis for what we will be looking at in verses 24-25. What does verse 24 say we are to consider? What are some ways that can be accomplished? **5.** What are those who are holding fast the confession of hope called *immediately* to do (v. 25)? **6.** When do you get together with other Christians? List all the other opportunities that you have for fellowship. In what ways do you need to be encouraged to meet together?

Pray: Ask God to give you a desire to be drawn into fellowship with other Christians. "If we walk in the light, as he is in the light, we have fellowship with one another" (1 Jn. 1:7).

QUIET TIME 2. GENUINE LOVE

Pray to the God of love, who out of his love has called us to meet together and love one another as he has loved us.

Read Romans 12:9-13. **1.** What quality is our love to have? What do you think this means? **2.** According to these verses, in what ways is this genuine love expressed? **3.** What does Paul mean in verse 10 when he told the Romans to "outdo one another in showing honor"? **4.** In what specific ways can you serve the Lord? **5.** What is your attitude toward tribulation, the troubles that come with being a Christian? How does that affect your relationship with others? **6.** How can you contribute to the needs of the saints (all true believers)? **7.** What are some ways you could practice hospitality?

Pray for the needs of others, asking God to show you ways to meet those needs. Pray specifically that you can begin showing genuine love to others in the ways you've listed.

QUIET TIME 3. UNITY

Pray: Confess your sins to God, particularly where you have sinned against others. With the air clear, ask him to be your guide as he brings you to his knowledge of unity.

Read Ephesians 4:1-6. **1.** In verse 1, Paul exhorts us to lead a life worthy of our calling. How does he expand on this in verses 2-3? **2.** What does it mean to be lowly and meek? In what areas of your life do you need to be humble? **3.** Who are some Christians you are impatient with? Why? **4.** Forbearance means refraining from the enforcement of something such as payment of a debt or obligation. Why is forbearance important to us as Christians? What does love add to forbearance? **5.** How have you seen relationships hurt when you've stuck up for your "rights" or kept silent when someone has done you an injustice? **6.** In verses 4-6, what is our unity based on? **7.** How can *you* help maintain unity?

Pray: Ask God to make you eager to maintain the unity of the Spirit in the ways you've listed.

QUIET TIME 4. BEING OF ONE MIND
Pray that as God draws you to himself in this quiet time that he will show you ways that you can be drawn closer to other Christians.

Read Philippians 2:1-4. **1.** What characteristics of all true Christians does Paul give in verse 1? **2.** Verse 1 refers to our relationship with God. To whom is Paul referring in the rest of these verses? Why is verse 1 important before moving on to the rest of the passage? **3.** How does Paul say the Philippians can make his joy complete (v. 2)? **4.** What does it mean to be of the same mind? **5.** How can we maintain the same love? **6.** How does Paul say in verses 3-4 that this unity can be fostered? **7.** In what ways are you often selfish? **8.** Paul is not saying that others *are* better than we are but that we should act toward them *as if* they were. This goes against our human nature. Nonetheless, why is it important to do this to maintain unity? **9.** Whom do you need to regard as more important than yourself? How can you do that? **10.** In what other ways do you need to stop being selfish?

Pray that God will give you a self-sacrificial attitude which will enable you to put others first. Pray specifically that God will change you accordingly as you answered the last two questions.

QUIET TIME 5. ENCOURAGING ONE ANOTHER

Pray that God will teach you how to encourage others in Christ.

Read 1 Thessalonians 5:11-15. **1.** What does Paul challenge the Thessalonians to do in verse 11?

2. In the remaining verses Paul teaches them how to do this. What are we to do according to verses 12-13 to build up the Christian leaders who are over us? **3.** How do you feel about the Christians who have charge over you? How do you respond when you are given instruction by an older Christian? **4.** How can you show respect to and highly esteem those over you? **5.** What four things does Paul urge us to do for other fellow Christians (v. 14)? **6.** How do you feel about admonishing (indicating obligations or expressing disapproval in a gentle manner) an idle believer? **7.** How can you encourage the fainthearted (timid)? Whom do you know who is weak and how can you help? **8.** When admonishing, encouraging or helping, what do we need? **9.** What does Paul tell us always to do (v. 15)?

Pray for patience as you seek to encourage the Christians who came to mind in this study.

Further reading: The Mark of the Christian by Francis Schaeffer (IVP); *Three Kinds of Love* by Masumi Toyotome (IVP) and *Life Together* by Dietrich Bonhoeffer (Harper & Row).

WEEK 4
MINISTRY

QUIET TIME 1. BUILDING UP THE BODY
Pray: Ask God to teach you what ministry is.
Read Ephesians 4:1, 11-16. **1.** What does Paul entreat us to do as Christians (v. 1)? **2.** In verse 11 there is a list of vocations to which God has called different people. Verse 7 teaches that we all have at least one gift though it is not necessarily listed in verse 11 (or any of the other lists Paul gives). What is the final result of these services according to verse 12? **3.** Verse 13 explains more fully "the building up of the body of Christ." List each goal of building up the body. **4.** Unity, knowledge, and maturity are the results of people ministering to one another. As verses 7 and 11-13 teach, we are all ministers for one another. Take a minute and jot down some ways that people have ministered to you by helping you achieve these goals. **5.** In verse 15 it says "we are to grow up in every way into him who is the head, into Christ." What is our primary motive for

helping the body grow (v. 16)? **6.** What does verse 16 teach about each individual's responsibility? **7.** Now write a definition of ministry.

Pray: Ask God to open you up to the gifts and talents that you can use to minister to others for the building up of the body of Christ.

QUIET TIME 2. DISCOVERING OUR GIFTS

Pray: Ask for the Holy Spirit's presence and for God's forgiveness for anything standing between you and him. **1.** Today we will explore how to determine your gifts. You must be open to the possibility of having several gifts, having gifts not listed in the Bible (such as taking care of small children, singing, sports), of having small, quiet gifts, or of having gifts that will require a great deal of development. **2.** Write down answers to these questions: What talents do people compliment you on? What do you like to do? What do you do well? What do you feel needs special attention in your church or Christian fellowship? In what activities have others benefited spiritually because of your efforts? **3.** How can you gather more information on how you could use these gifts or whether or not these really are your gifts? What close friend would be willing to give an objective and sensitive review of your gifts? **4.** Review your list of gifts and ask yourself these questions: Which gifts or talents am I willing to use in ministry to others? Does sin in my life restrict God from using any? If so, which ones? Do I continually tell God that I am dependent on his supernatural working to transform my efforts for the good of his church?

Pray: Put the possibilities listed in question 2 on your prayer list for the next week. Pray that God will guide you in their development.

QUIET TIME 3. GIFTS FOR THE COMMON GOOD

Pray that you will be open to learn how your gifts may be used for the body of Christ.

Read 1 Corinthians 12:1-11. **1.** According to verse 3, what very important ability does the Holy Spirit give us? **2.** What contrast is made in verses 4-7 in three slightly different ways? For what purpose is the working of the Spirit given? **3.** Verses 8-10 give one of the lists of spiritual gifts found in Scripture (though no one list is exhaustive since all are different). How might each of these contribute to the common good of the body of Christ? **4.** Who gives the gifts (v. 11)? How can you grow in your dependence on the Spirit for the working of his will through you?

Pray: Gifts grow and develop as we use them.

Our gifts become clearer to us as we seek to serve Christ and the church. Dedicate your gifts to God, asking him to use them as he sees fit in the body of Christ.

QUIET TIME 4. MANY MEMBERS, ONE BODY

Pray: Ask God to show you how you can best use your gifts and understand your limits so that you may see the need for and encourage the use of others' gifts.

Read 1 Corinthians 12:12-26. **1.** Whose body is Paul speaking of? What is the body made up of? **2.** How do people differ from one another in your church or fellowship? How do they differ from you? **3.** What would be the problems if there were no differences, if we were all the same (vv. 17-20)? **4.** What attitude is Paul opposed to in verse 21? How have you been expressing a similar attitude? **5.** The body is put together in such a way that we need one another. How do people use their gifts to help you? **6.** With these differences in mind, why can you say with certainty that you are all members of one body? **7.** What results if one member suffers or is honored? When have you suffered or rejoiced with another recently?

Pray: Thank God for the gifts of others.

QUIET TIME 5. MINISTRY WORLDWIDE

Pray that God will give you a vision for how he is working worldwide to build his church.

Read Matthew 28:18-20. Here Christ is teaching the disciples what he wants them to do now that he has died and has risen from the dead. **1.** What four commands does Jesus give the disciples? **2.** Where are they to go? **3.** Making disciples is more than just helping people become Christians. What else do you think is involved? **4.** On what basis does Jesus give such a large task to the disciples (v. 18)? **5.** What does he offer to help them fulfill the task (v. 20)? **6.** What do you know of what God is doing in other nations? How can you find out more? **7.** God calls all his people to build up his body worldwide. He may be calling you to help in your current location or he may be calling you to go to another country. What can you do in your current locale to build up the worldwide body of Christ? How may he be calling you to use your gifts in another nation or culture? **8.** If you do not know where God wants you to serve, what can you do to begin seeking his guidance?

Pray: Ask God if he wants you to use your gifts in another culture.

Further reading: By the Power of the Holy Spirit by David M. Howard (IVP).

WEEK 5
PRIORITIES

QUIET TIME 1. PRESSURES

Pray: Ask God to help you understand what your priorities in life should be.

Read Mark 1:21-39. **1.** What activities was Jesus involved in in Capernaum? **2.** What demands were placed on him? **3.** Why would it make sense for him to stay in Capernaum rather than leave? **4.** What did he say was his priority (v. 38)? **5.** How did Jesus decide what he should do? **6.** What evidence is there that it was Jesus' routine to rise early and pray? **7.** What role does prayer have as you set your priorities? **8.** What steps can you take to give prayer itself a higher priority in your life?

Pray that God will help you set your priorities this week through close and continued contact with him through prayer.

QUIET TIME 2. POSSESSIONS

Pray: Ask the Holy Spirit to show you where your attitudes toward possessions need to be changed.

Read 1 Timothy 6:6-10. **1.** In what ways is godliness a means of great gain? **2.** What does it mean to be content? **3.** In verse 7 what does Paul say about acquiring wealth on earth? **4.** What should be all that is needed to keep us content? If you had to give up everything, except food and clothing, how would you feel? **5.** According to verse 9, what happens to those who desire wealth? **6.** How can being rich lead to foolish and harmful desires? What are some of your foolish or harmful desires? **7.** Which are keeping you from being satisfied with God? What do you need to do about that?

Pray: Ask God to give you the strength to give up those things which are keeping you from being satisfied with him and to draw into a deeper relationship with him.

QUIET TIME 3. TRUST

Pray: Thank God for this time and ask him to guide you in discovering the attitude you should have toward your needs.

Read Matthew 6:25-34. **1.** In your notebook, list in a column what Jesus tells us not to worry about. In a second column, list next to each item the reason why we shouldn't worry about it. **2.** Verse 32 states that God knows everything we need. Look up *need* and *want* in a dictionary, and write out the definitions you find. What difference is there between the two? **3.** What does it mean to seek first "his kingdom and his righteousness"? What is the result of seeking first his kingdom? **4.** What do you need? How does this passage affect your attitude toward your needs? **5.** List five things that you spend time worrying about. **6.** In what ways are you seeking his kingdom?

Pray: Ask God to change your attitude toward the things you are worrying about. Pray that he will help you focus your energies on his concerns first.

QUIET TIME 4. CONTENT IN CIRCUMSTANCES

Pray: Ask God to help you examine your attitudes toward him as a result of the situations he has placed you in.

Read Philippians 4:11-13. **1.** According to verse 12, what circumstances has Paul experienced? **2.** What is Paul's attitude in the midst of these circumstances according to verse 11? **3.** What part does God play in his attitudes? (See also Heb. 13:5.) **4.** What part does God play in your attitudes in the midst of adverse situations? **5.** What did Paul learn about his relationship to God in those adverse situations? In what circumstances has God placed you now? What is your attitude in these situations? What role does God play in your attitude? (Think: How satisfied are you with your material possessions—clothes, albums, plants and so on?) **6.** Memorize verse 13 and take it with you today.

Pray: Pray that throughout the day God will give you an attitude of contentment in your circumstances.

QUIET TIME 5. PRIORITIES FOR CHRIST'S PEOPLE

Pray that God will teach you his agenda for your life.

In John 15 Jesus summarizes his priorities for the disciples. Jesus is about to die and return to the Father and this is part of his final, important teaching for the disciples. It is his instruction about how we are to function as his followers. **1.** Read John 15:1-11. What does it mean to remain or abide in Jesus? How can you abide in Jesus in the 20th century? **2.** What does it mean to bear fruit? **3.** What does Jesus teach in verse 10? **4.** Read John 15:12-17. What does Jesus command in this section? **5.** Whom does he refer to when he says, "one another"? **6.** The quality of our love for fellow believers is to be the same as the quality of love that Jesus has for us. How did Jesus show his love to us? What does that imply about our love for others? **7.** Read John 15:26-27. What does Jesus say we are in verse 27? **8.** What comfort does he give the disciples as they fulfill this task? **9.** Bearing witness to Jesus means sharing the good news of Christ with the world. It also means social involvement. Read Matthew 25:31-40. How would you describe this social responsibility to the world? **10.** Jesus leaves his disciples with three main priorities: (1.) Our personal relationship with Jesus Christ (abiding and obeying); (2.) Our relationship with other Christians (love each other); and (3.) Our relationship to the world (evangelism and social responsibility). Tomorrow these truths will be applied to your lifestyle.

Pray that God will remind you of his priorities today and that you will be open to more carefully applying them to your life tomorrow.

QUIET TIME 6. LIVING BIBLICAL PRIORITIES

Pray that God the Holy Spirit will apply his biblical priorities to your life.

1. Review the priorities that you studied yesterday in John 15. **2.** This quiet time is mainly application of the truths that you learned yesterday. (1.) Do you allow time daily for your relationship with Jesus Christ in Bible study and prayer? (2.) Do you allow time each week for fellowship and worship with other Christians? for ministry to other Christians? for your family? (3.) Do you allow time for ministry to the world including evangelism and involvement? **3.** Divide up a whole page of your notebook into the days of the week. Now try to write a schedule which reflects biblical priorities. **4.** This is a good activity to work through weekly to ensure that you are living according to biblical priorities.

Pray for the comfort and counsel of the Holy Spirit as you attempt to live according to biblical priorities.

Further Reading: Sacrifice by Howard Guinness (IVP); *The Cost of Commitment* by John White (IVP).

WEEK 6
PERSONAL EVANGELISM

QUIET TIME 1. STEPS TO SALVATION
Pray that God will show you the importance of sharing your faith with others.

Read Romans 10:13-17. **1.** What questions are asked in verses 14-15? Use one word to describe each step in the process of a person coming to Christ. **2.** What is the final result of sending, preaching, hearing, believing and calling on the name of the Lord (v. 13)? **3.** What does "being saved" or "salvation" mean to you? What do you think you were saved from? **4.** How does one acquire faith according to verse 17? **5.** God has entrusted the task of evangelism, or sharing the good news of Jesus Christ, with every Christian. What would happen if no Christians shared the message of Jesus Christ with anyone? **6.** Who shared the word of Christ with you? Thank God for that person's love and concern for you. Perhaps you can write that person a note thanking him or her for sharing Jesus Christ with you. **7.** What relationships do you have with non-Christians with whom you can share the message of Jesus Christ? Jot down their names on your prayer list and begin praying regularly for them.

QUIET TIME 2. A COMMON INTEREST

Pray: Ask God to make you aware of effective ways to establish friendships with non-Christians.

Read John 4:1-8. **1.** Jesus, on his way to Galilee, was passing through Samaria. Why did he stop by the well? Who else came to the well? **2.** Jesus has just made a social contact with this Samaritan woman on her own ground. What does this imply about Christians and their contacts with non-Christians? List all of the places where you have contact with non-Christians. **3.** Why did the woman come to the well? What did Jesus ask her to do? What was the common interest that was established between Jesus and the woman? **4.** One of the best ways to get to know someone is to share a common interest. What are your interests? (Don't forget ordinary interests like your living situation, your country and so on.) **5.** Looking over your lists of interests and of places you have contact with non-Christians, can you think of any opportunities that you may have to get to know more non-Christians?

Pray specifically for the people that you listed yesterday. Also pray for new contacts and deeper friendships with non-Christians.

QUIET TIME 3. GUIDING CONVERSATIONS

Pray: Confess your sins to the all holy God. Thank him for his forgiveness and ask him to teach you.

Read John 4:9-12. **1.** Why does it surprise the woman that Jesus has spoken to her? What barriers do you need to break with non-Christians? **2.** In verse 10 Jesus continues to arouse her interest. What does Jesus offer the woman? **3.** How does the woman show that she is interested? Jesus makes a statement that demands a response. He turns the conversation from a known interest to one's relationship with God. In yesterday's quiet time you listed some of your interests. How are each of them related to Christianity? **4.** Read John 4:13-15. Where does this water come from? **5.** What is unique about this water that he has to give? **6.** Who is Jesus revealing to her in this analogy of water? Who should be the center of our discussions with non-Christians? **7.** Jesus is gradually revealing himself to the woman as she becomes ready for more. How does the woman's reply show that she is ready to receive more of his message? How can we know when our friends are ready for more of the message?

Pray: Ask God to help lead your conversations into discussions about Jesus Christ, and for the sensitivity not to go further than you should.

QUIET TIME 4. FOCUSING ON CHRIST

Pray: Ask God to search your heart and cleanse it as you learn about sharing his love.

Read John 4:16-19. **1.** What do we learn about the woman in these verses? **2.** Being God, Jesus knew the woman's sins. Why did he ask her to go and get her husband? What must a person be made aware of before they can see their need for salvation? **3.** In the conversation the woman's sins are made apparent but Jesus never condemns her. What are some ways that we may help non-Christians see their own sinfulness without condemning them? **4.** Read verses 20-26. The woman is getting sidetracked by putting an emphasis on where to worship. What does Jesus emphasize in verse 23? How does this steer the conversation back to his message? **5.** What are some questions that non-Christians ask that lead to discussions of secondary issues? How could you turn the discussion back to Christ? **6.** Who is the woman looking for to teach her how to worship? How does Jesus' response present her with a decision? **7.** Jesus' final response is a direct confrontation of himself with the woman—she must decide for or against him. When we have presented the whole gospel, we must bring the non-Christian to a direct confrontation with Jesus Christ so that he or she realizes his or her personal responsibility to make a decision. What are some ways that you could confront your non-Christian friends? **8.** How important are your prayers at this time? **9.** A conversation such as this may not take place all at once but over a period of weeks, months or even years. What is the importance of patience in a friendship when results are slow?

Pray: Ask God to help you not be condemning toward non-Christians; to stick to the main topic—the gospel; and to confront them with the responsibility to make a decision for Christ.

QUIET TIME 5. FOLLOW UP

Pray: Clear the air with God and ask him to draw you closer to him in this time.

Read Philippians 1:3-11. **1.** In verses 3-4 Paul speaks of one of the most important ways in which we are to support new Christians. What is it? **2.** What should our attitude in prayer be? **3.** What is Paul confident of in verse 6? Why? **4.** In verse 7, what fellowship does Paul have with the Philippians? How can we encourage a young Christian to have fellowship? **5.** In Philippians 1:9 Paul says he is praying for their lives to have several qualities. What are they? Looking back on your own Christian life what are some ways that you have grown in love, knowledge and discernment? **6.** What are the results of prayer, fellowship and Bible study (vv. 10-11)? Who gives us the power to do these things? Who deserves the glory? **7.** How has God worked in your life to help you grow as a Christian? through whom? **8.** Think of a younger Christian with whom you can share some fundamentals of the Christian life (prayer, fellowship, quiet time, God's will, ministry and so on.) What are some steps that you can take to accomplish this?

Pray: Thank God for all that he has taught you about evangelism. Ask that he'll give you the power to put this knowledge to work. Also pray that he'll guide you to a younger Christian with whom you can share the things you've been learning.

Further reading: For your own understanding of the gospel of Jesus Christ, *Becoming a Christian* by John R. W. Stott (IVP) contains a brief and clear summary of the Christian message. For more help in sharing Christ: *How to Give Away Your Faith* by Paul E. Little (IVP) and *The Gospel in a Pagan Society* by Kenneth Prior (IVP).

WEEK 7
GOD'S WILL

QUIET TIME 1. THE SCRIPTURES
Pray: Ask God to make you expectant and eager to learn from him this morning.

Read Exodus 20:1-17. **1.** List ten major statements of God's will for the lives of his people. **2.** Read Romans 12:1-21. List at least twenty more directives for Christian living. **3.** How does Paul summarize the purposes and uses of Scripture in 2 Timothy 3:16-17. **4.** Since most of God's will is already revealed to us in the Bible, what should our attitude be in coming to the Scriptures? **5.** What is a realistic amount of time to spend daily in Bible study? **6.** When is the best time of day for you to schedule in this time? **7.** Where in your life are you failing to act on what you already know of God's will?

Pray: Thank God for providing the Scriptures. Ask him to help you act on his revealed will.

QUIET TIME 2. ATTITUDES NEEDED FOR GUIDANCE

Pray: Ask that God will make you teachable this morning—open and alert to his voice.

Read Psalm 25:1-15. **1.** Look through the whole passage carefully. What kind of person receives instruction and favor from the Lord? **2.** What does David ask for? What do these requests show about his attitudes toward God? **3.** Where do your attitudes toward God need changing? (Do you possess patient trust in God? A desire to know God's will? A deep desire to turn from old sins and do God's will? Obedience to his will? "Eyes... ever toward the LORD"?) **4.** What are some ways you can work to change those attitudes?

Pray: Ask God to do the changing from the inside through the Holy Spirit. Ask him to continue to show you his will for you, a little at a time.

QUIET TIME 3. FEELINGS AND CIRCUMSTANCES

Pray: Greet God and ask him to supply his Holy Spirit to guide you into truth regarding his will.

Read Acts 20:17-25, 36-38. **1.** What qualities characterize Paul's ministry (vv. 18-21)? **2.** What is Paul's ministry and from whom did he get it (v. 24)? **3.** How did Paul react to the difficult circumstances he encountered while carrying out God's will for his life (see Acts 19:21-41 and 20:20-21)? **4.** Where was Paul going next (v. 22)? **5.** What problems are ahead in Jerusalem (v. 23)? **6.** How would you have felt about the prospects of making a trip like this one? **7.** How did Paul's friends react? Why didn't their great sorrow dissuade Paul from going to Jerusalem? **8.** What kinds of circumstances other than the reactions of friends might cause us to draw back from following God's will (such as, money considerations, possible embarassment and so on)? **9.** What kind of attitude should replace desires for personal comfort, or safety or the rebellious desire for self-direction (v. 24)? **10.** Where are you most susceptible to disobedience because you don't feel like obeying or because circumstances look difficult? (Think of your personal struggles with the many commands listed in this week's first quiet time.) **11.** What are some of your most frequently used excuses for not acting on God's revealed will (such as, "I've never done that before," "That's for fanatics," "I'm not that disciplined" or "I don't have time")? What do you need to act on without further delay?

Pray: Ask God to make you aware of your excuses and to make you able to love him enough to obey even when you don't feel like it.

QUIET TIME 4. MAKING DECISIONS

Pray: Ask God to be with you now.

Read Acts 15:1-29. **1.** This is the first serious conflict for the early Christian church. What is happening in verses 4-7? What facts were being gathered? **2.** How would it be difficult to make a wise decision if you weren't able to see as many facts as possible? **3.** At the council they heard both sides of the issue. What can be learned from this? **4.** What are some things which hinder us from knowing all possible alternatives? **5.** In verses 13-21 James takes control of the situation. He states the facts, but then where does he turn? **6.** How should the Scriptures affect our decisions? **7.** Before coming to a decision James heard from the Pharisees, Peter, Paul, Barnabas and probably many others. Why is it important to seek out others for help in making decisions? **8.** Why do we often resist the advice of others? **9.** After all was said and done, what did James do (v. 19)? **10.** How did the counsel act on the decision (vv. 22-29)? Why is it important to do something after a decision is made? **11.** Where are you seeking God's will? How can you come to a decision?

Pray: Ask God for his guidance for you.

Further reading: Affirming the Will of God by Paul E. Little (IVP), *Guidance* by Barclay (IVP).

WEEK 8
QUIET TIMES

QUIET TIME 1. GOD REVEALS HIMSELF

Pray: A quiet time is the time you spend alone with God, receiving private instruction and talking with him. As you begin each quiet time invite the Lord to be present with you, acknowledge who it is you are talking to—the Lord of the Universe—and clear any barriers caused by sin. Do this now.

Read Psalm 19:1-6. **1.** The desire of every Christian is to know God. These verses tell us about one way God has revealed himself to us—through nature. What does the sky tell us about God? **2.** How is the sun described here? **3.** What do the characteristics of creation tell us about the Creator? **4.** Read Psalm 19:7-10. The terms *law, precept, ordinance, commandment* and *testimony* all refer to God's written Word. They reveal far more to us about God than nature does. In verses 7-9 find five descriptions of the law and five effects of each aspect of God's written testimony. **5.** These five effects of the law lead the writer of this Psalm to what conclusions in verse 10? **6.** Read Psalm 19:11-14. What use does the law have (v. 11)? What reward? **7.** What does the psalmist ask in verses 12-13? **8.** Words are outward expressions and meditations are inward thoughts. What is the psalmist's greatest desire? **9.** After meeting with God and thinking about their relationship, how does the psalmist name the Lord? Why are the names in the last line important?

Pray verses 12-14 for yourself and pray that God will reveal to you more about himself daily.

QUIET TIME 2. BIBLE STUDY
Pray: Ask God for alertness and openness to learning how to study his Word.

Read James 1:19-25. **1.** How are the readers of this letter addressed? **2.** What are they commanded to do (vv. 19-21)? **3.** What do your answers to questions 1 and 2 tell you about James's attitude toward his readers? **4.** What three key commands are given in verses 21-22? **5.** How can the first step be obeyed in a quiet time? **6.** How can our attitudes be changed as we begin quiet times to match those required in the second step? **7.** What does verse 22 say about the results of our time spent with God? How can you be a doer?

8. Look at the illustration in verses 23-25. How would you describe the man who looked in the mirror? **9.** How is a mirror like the law of the Lord? **10.** What is the result promised to those who act on what they have learned?

Pray that God will enable you to be a doer of the Word and not merely a hearer.

QUIET TIME 3. PRAYER

Quiet times are the key to a close personal relationship with God. Prayer is one of the most important keys to good quiet times. David had an intimate relationship with God, so looking at Psalm 86 as a prayer in difficult times will show us what is important in prayer. Look for his attitudes.

Read Psalm 86. **1.** Now underline all the "I" pronouns and the "you" or "thou" pronouns.

Pray that God will help you have such a close relationship with him.

2. How does David describe himself in verses 1-7? **3.** How does he describe God? **4.** What does he ask? **5.** What fraction of the prayer is devoted to this conscious recognition of David's relationship to God and the invitation for God to meet with David? **6.** Now look at verses 8-10. What do you notice about all the pronouns you underlined? This is an excellent example of adoration.

David acknowledges who God is and that he is worthy of praise. **7.** What does David ask in verses 11-13? **8.** Why would he make these requests? (How does he view himself?) **9.** David is honest and open with God about his shortcomings and needs. What do verses 12-13 tell you about why David can feel so open? **10.** In what ways are you aware of his steadfast love? of his deliverance? **11.** In verses 14-17 David comes to his reason for prayer. What is his problem? **12.** What fraction of this prayer is devoted to the request for help in this life-and-death matter? **13.** Summarize the different kinds of prayer in this Psalm?

Pray: Take plenty of time to pray a complete prayer using David's prayer as a guide.

QUIET TIME 4. AN EXAMPLE

Pray: Invite God to be with you and to enrich you with his presence.

Read Mark 10:23-31. (In quiet times you should always choose a passage that is short enough to be covered thoroughly, but long enough to teach you several new things.) **1.** *What is the passage basically about?* Ask yourself such questions as—Who was speaking? Who else was there? How might those people have felt? What would the disciples have had to leave behind? How would you have felt? Why? **2.** *What does it teach about God?* Consider the following questions and any others that come to mind. What is he able to do? What sort of people does he favor? How does he reward self-sacrificing people? **3.** *What does it teach about life?* How do the standards that we will actually be measured by differ from the standards that the world tries to apply to us? **4.** *Is there a command or a warning for me?* Look at verse 24b. What is the warning? Look at verses 29-30. What promises are made? **5.** *Is there an example to follow or an error to avoid?* Look at verse 28. **6.** *How does this apply to my life and how can I put it into practice?* In what ways are you rich? How could that make you unable to fit into the kingdom? With your own circumstances, how can you follow Peter's example? Be specific. **7.** *Write down what you feel to be particularly important about this passage as God's practical application for you today.* (A passage can be applied many ways: make a list of things to praise or thank God for; confess new awareness of a sin; note relationships to continue, change or start.)

Pray: Ask God to help you and thank him for his teachings. (Put the seven questions on a note card and keep it in your Bible. If you begin and end your quiet time with prayer, these questions can be a useful guide for studying any passage.)

QUIET TIME 5. DISCIPLINE

Good quiet times—like everything else—take practice and discipline. Don't be afraid to innovate. Since these are your personal times with God you can count on him being flexible enough to meet your needs in ways unique to you. Ask others about their quiet times and try a variety of techniques, but be sure to give each a fair try and a thorough evaluation. Check with pastors, friends or parents for passages that will suit your interests or problems.

Pray: Put away all distracting thoughts and concentrate on the One with whom you are spending this time.

Read Isaiah 11:1-5. **1.** What is the passage basically about? **2.** What does it teach about God? **3.** What does it teach about life? **4.** Is there a command, a promise or a warning? **5.** Is there an example to follow or an error to avoid? **6.** How does it apply to my life, and how can I put it into practice? **7.** What is the most important thing you have learned here? Exactly how will you apply this lesson? Is there a topic for further study here?

Pray: Speak directly to God as he has been more fully revealed to you today. Share your plans for today with him. Are they his plans too?

Further reading: Quiet Time (IVP).